800+ Measurable IEP Goals and Objectives

Goal Tracker and Progress Report for IEP Goals

Chris de Feyter MEd., MSc.

© 2014

Today's Date		Start time		End time	
Who worked with the student? (name)			○ Intervention Teacher ○ Classroom Teacher ○ Assistant ○ Administrator ○ Social Worker ○ Occupational Therapist ○ Physiotherapist ○ Speech Pathologist ○ Psychologist ○ Other, _____		
SMART Goal #	○ 1 ○ 2 ○ 3 ○ 4 ○ 5 ○ 6 ○ 7 ○ 8 ○ 9 ○ 10	Short Term Learning Objective	○ 1 ○ 2 ○ 3 ○ 4	Objective or goal met? ○ Y ○ N	

Briefly describe instructional Strategy

Level of Performance (how well did the student perform the activity, from 1 *poor* to 5 *very good*)	○ 1 ○ 2 ○ 3 ○ 4 ○ 5

Briefly describe observed strengths, successes and / or growth

What would you do differently when doing a similar activity related to the above SMART goal, to give the student more opportunities to progress?

What can the Parents / Guardians do at home to support this goal?

Anecdotal Notes and Comments from School Staff

Anecdotal Notes and Comments from Parents / Guardians

Page _____

Today's Date		Start time		End time	
Who worked with the student? (name)			○ Intervention Teacher ○ Classroom Teacher ○ Assistant ○ Administrator ○ Social Worker ○ Occupational Therapist ○ Physiotherapist ○ Speech Pathologist ○ Psychologist ○ Other, _____		
SMART Goal #	○1 ○2 ○3 ○4 ○5 ○6 ○7 ○8 ○9 ○10	Short Term Learning Objective	○1 ○2 ○3 ○4	Objective or goal met?	○Y ○N

Briefly describe instructional Strategy

Level of Performance (how well did the student perform the activity, from 1 *poor* to 5 *very good*)	○1 ○2 ○3 ○4 ○5

Briefly describe observed strengths, successes and / or growth

What would you do differently when doing a similar activity related to the above SMART goal, to give the student more opportunities to progress?

What can the Parents / Guardians do at home to support this goal?

Anecdotal Notes and Comments from School Staff

Anecdotal Notes and Comments from Parents / Guardians

Today's Date		Start time		End time	
Who worked with the student? (name)		○ Intervention Teacher ○ Classroom Teacher ○ Assistant ○ Administrator ○ Social Worker ○ Occupational Therapist ○ Physiotherapist ○ Speech Pathologist ○ Psychologist ○ Other, _____			
SMART Goal #	○ 1 ○ 2 ○ 3 ○ 4 ○ 5 ○ 6 ○ 7 ○ 8 ○ 9 ○ 10	Short Term Learning Objective	○ 1 ○ 2 ○ 3 ○ 4	Objective or goal met?	○ Y ○ N

Briefly describe instructional Strategy

Level of Performance (how well did the student perform the activity, from 1 *poor* to 5 *very good*)	○ 1 ○ 2 ○ 3 ○ 4 ○ 5

Briefly describe observed strengths, successes and / or growth

What would you do differently when doing a similar activity related to the above SMART goal, to give the student more opportunities to progress?

What can the Parents / Guardians do at home to support this goal?

Anecdotal Notes and Comments from School Staff

Anecdotal Notes and Comments from Parents / Guardians

Page _____

Today's Date		Start time		End time	
Who worked with the student? (name)			○ Intervention Teacher ○ Classroom Teacher ○ Assistant ○ Administrator ○ Social Worker ○ Occupational Therapist ○ Physiotherapist ○ Speech Pathologist ○ Psychologist ○ Other, _____		
SMART Goal #	○ 1 ○ 2 ○ 3 ○ 4 ○ 5 ○ 6 ○ 7 ○ 8 ○ 9 ○ 10	Short Term Learning Objective	○ 1 ○ 2 ○ 3 ○ 4	Objective or goal met? ○ Y ○ N	

Briefly describe instructional Strategy

Level of Performance (how well did the student perform the activity, from 1 *poor* to 5 *very good*)	○ 1 ○ 2 ○ 3 ○ 4 ○ 5

Briefly describe observed strengths, successes and / or growth

What would you do differently when doing a similar activity related to the above SMART goal, to give the student more opportunities to progress?

What can the Parents / Guardians do at home to support this goal?

Anecdotal Notes and Comments from School Staff

Anecdotal Notes and Comments from Parents / Guardians

Page _____

Today's Date		Start time		End time	
Who worked with the student? (name)			○ Intervention Teacher ○ Classroom Teacher ○ Assistant ○ Administrator ○ Social Worker ○ Occupational Therapist ○ Physiotherapist ○ Speech Pathologist ○ Psychologist ○ Other, _____		
SMART Goal #	○ 1 ○ 2 ○ 3 ○ 4 ○ 5 ○ 6 ○ 7 ○ 8 ○ 9 ○ 10	Short Term Learning Objective	○ 1 ○ 2 ○ 3 ○ 4	Objective or goal met? ○ Y ○ N	

Briefly describe instructional Strategy

Level of Performance (how well did the student perform the activity, from 1 *poor* to 5 *very good*)	○ 1 ○ 2 ○ 3 ○ 4 ○ 5

Briefly describe observed strengths, successes and / or growth

What would you do differently when doing a similar activity related to the above SMART goal, to give the student more opportunities to progress?

What can the Parents / Guardians do at home to support this goal?

Anecdotal Notes and Comments from School Staff

Anecdotal Notes and Comments from Parents / Guardians

Page _____

Today's Date		Start time		End time	
Who worked with the student? (name)			○ Intervention Teacher ○ Classroom Teacher ○ Assistant ○ Administrator ○ Social Worker ○ Occupational Therapist ○ Physiotherapist ○ Speech Pathologist ○ Psychologist ○ Other, _____		
SMART Goal #	○ 1 ○ 2 ○ 3 ○ 4 ○ 5 ○ 6 ○ 7 ○ 8 ○ 9 ○ 10	Short Term Learning Objective	○ 1 ○ 2 ○ 3 ○ 4	Objective or goal met? ○ Y ○ N	

Briefly describe instructional Strategy

Level of Performance (how well did the student perform the activity, from 1 *poor* to 5 *very good*)	○ 1 ○ 2 ○ 3 ○ 4 ○ 5

Briefly describe observed strengths, successes and / or growth

What would you do differently when doing a similar activity related to the above SMART goal, to give the student more opportunities to progress?

What can the Parents / Guardians do at home to support this goal?

Anecdotal Notes and Comments from School Staff

Anecdotal Notes and Comments from Parents / Guardians

Page _____

Today's Date		Start time		End time	
Who worked with the student? (name)			○ Intervention Teacher ○ Classroom Teacher ○ Assistant ○ Administrator ○ Social Worker ○ Occupational Therapist ○ Physiotherapist ○ Speech Pathologist ○ Psychologist ○ Other, _____		
SMART Goal #	○ 1 ○ 2 ○ 3 ○ 4 ○ 5 ○ 6 ○ 7 ○ 8 ○ 9 ○ 10	Short Term Learning Objective	○ 1 ○ 2 ○ 3 ○ 4	Objective or goal met? ○ Y ○ N	

Briefly describe instructional Strategy

Level of Performance (how well did the student perform the activity, from 1 *poor* to 5 *very good*)	○ 1 ○ 2 ○ 3 ○ 4 ○ 5

Briefly describe observed strengths, successes and / or growth

What would you do differently when doing a similar activity related to the above SMART goal, to give the student more opportunities to progress?

What can the Parents / Guardians do at home to support this goal?

Anecdotal Notes and Comments from School Staff

Anecdotal Notes and Comments from Parents / Guardians

Page _____

Today's Date		Start time		End time	
Who worked with the student? (name)			○ Intervention Teacher ○ Classroom Teacher ○ Assistant ○ Administrator ○ Social Worker ○ Occupational Therapist ○ Physiotherapist ○ Speech Pathologist ○ Psychologist ○ Other, _____		
SMART Goal #	○ 1 ○ 2 ○ 3 ○ 4 ○ 5 ○ 6 ○ 7 ○ 8 ○ 9 ○ 10	Short Term Learning Objective	○ 1 ○ 2 ○ 3 ○ 4	Objective or goal met?	○ Y ○ N

Briefly describe instructional Strategy

Level of Performance (how well did the student perform the activity, from 1 *poor* to 5 *very good*)　　○ 1 ○ 2 ○ 3 ○ 4 ○ 5

Briefly describe observed strengths, successes and / or growth

What would you do differently when doing a similar activity related to the above SMART goal, to give the student more opportunities to progress?

What can the Parents / Guardians do at home to support this goal?

Anecdotal Notes and Comments from School Staff

Anecdotal Notes and Comments from Parents / Guardians

Today's Date		Start time		End time	
Who worked with the student? (name)			○ Intervention Teacher ○ Classroom Teacher ○ Assistant ○ Administrator ○ Social Worker ○ Occupational Therapist ○ Physiotherapist ○ Speech Pathologist ○ Psychologist ○ Other, _____		
SMART Goal #	○ 1 ○ 2 ○ 3 ○ 4 ○ 5 ○ 6 ○ 7 ○ 8 ○ 9 ○ 10	Short Term Learning Objective	○ 1 ○ 2 ○ 3 ○ 4	Objective or goal met? ○ Y ○ N	

Briefly describe instructional Strategy

Level of Performance (how well did the student perform the activity, from 1 *poor* to 5 *very good*)	○ 1 ○ 2 ○ 3 ○ 4 ○ 5

Briefly describe observed strengths, successes and / or growth

What would you do differently when doing a similar activity related to the above SMART goal, to give the student more opportunities to progress?

What can the Parents / Guardians do at home to support this goal?

Anecdotal Notes and Comments from School Staff

Anecdotal Notes and Comments from Parents / Guardians

Today's Date		Start time		End time	
Who worked with the student? (name)			○ Intervention Teacher ○ Classroom Teacher ○ Assistant ○ Administrator ○ Social Worker ○ Occupational Therapist ○ Physiotherapist ○ Speech Pathologist ○ Psychologist ○ Other, _____		
SMART Goal #	○ 1 ○ 2 ○ 3 ○ 4 ○ 5 ○ 6 ○ 7 ○ 8 ○ 9 ○ 10	Short Term Learning Objective	○ 1 ○ 2 ○ 3 ○ 4	Objective or goal met? ○ Y ○ N	

Briefly describe instructional Strategy

Level of Performance (how well did the student perform the activity, from 1 *poor* to 5 *very good*)	○ 1 ○ 2 ○ 3 ○ 4 ○ 5

Briefly describe observed strengths, successes and / or growth

What would you do differently when doing a similar activity related to the above SMART goal, to give the student more opportunities to progress?

What can the Parents / Guardians do at home to support this goal?

Anecdotal Notes and Comments from School Staff

Anecdotal Notes and Comments from Parents / Guardians

Page _____

Today's Date		Start time		End time	
Who worked with the student? (name)			○ Intervention Teacher ○ Classroom Teacher ○ Assistant ○ Administrator ○ Social Worker ○ Occupational Therapist ○ Physiotherapist ○ Speech Pathologist ○ Psychologist ○ Other, _____		
SMART Goal #	○ 1 ○ 2 ○ 3 ○ 4 ○ 5 ○ 6 ○ 7 ○ 8 ○ 9 ○ 10	Short Term Learning Objective	○ 1 ○ 2 ○ 3 ○ 4	Objective or goal met? ○ Y ○ N	

Briefly describe instructional Strategy

Level of Performance (how well did the student perform the activity, from 1 *poor* to 5 *very good*)	○ 1 ○ 2 ○ 3 ○ 4 ○ 5

Briefly describe observed strengths, successes and / or growth

What would you do differently when doing a similar activity related to the above SMART goal, to give the student more opportunities to progress?

What can the Parents / Guardians do at home to support this goal?

Anecdotal Notes and Comments from School Staff

Anecdotal Notes and Comments from Parents / Guardians

Page _____

Today's Date		Start time		End time	
Who worked with the student? (name)		○ Intervention Teacher ○ Classroom Teacher ○ Assistant ○ Administrator ○ Social Worker ○ Occupational Therapist ○ Physiotherapist ○ Speech Pathologist ○ Psychologist ○ Other, _____			
SMART Goal #	○ 1 ○ 2 ○ 3 ○ 4 ○ 5 ○ 6 ○ 7 ○ 8 ○ 9 ○ 10	Short Term Learning Objective	○ 1 ○ 2 ○ 3 ○ 4	Objective or goal met? ○ Y ○ N	

Briefly describe instructional Strategy

Level of Performance (how well did the student perform the activity, from 1 *poor* to 5 *very good*)	○ 1 ○ 2 ○ 3 ○ 4 ○ 5

Briefly describe observed strengths, successes and / or growth

What would you do differently when doing a similar activity related to the above SMART goal, to give the student more opportunities to progress?

What can the Parents / Guardians do at home to support this goal?

Anecdotal Notes and Comments from School Staff

Anecdotal Notes and Comments from Parents / Guardians

Page _____

Today's Date		Start time		End time	
Who worked with the student? (name)			○ Intervention Teacher ○ Classroom Teacher ○ Assistant ○ Administrator ○ Social Worker ○ Occupational Therapist ○ Physiotherapist ○ Speech Pathologist ○ Psychologist ○ Other, _____		
SMART Goal #	○ 1 ○ 2 ○ 3 ○ 4 ○ 5 ○ 6 ○ 7 ○ 8 ○ 9 ○ 10	Short Term Learning Objective	○ 1 ○ 2 ○ 3 ○ 4	Objective or goal met?	○ Y ○ N

Briefly describe instructional Strategy

Level of Performance (how well did the student perform the activity, from 1 *poor* to 5 *very good*)	○ 1 ○ 2 ○ 3 ○ 4 ○ 5

Briefly describe observed strengths, successes and / or growth

What would you do differently when doing a similar activity related to the above SMART goal, to give the student more opportunities to progress?

What can the Parents / Guardians do at home to support this goal?

Anecdotal Notes and Comments from School Staff

Anecdotal Notes and Comments from Parents / Guardians

Page _____

Today's Date			Start time			End time		
Who worked with the student? (name)					○ Intervention Teacher ○ Classroom Teacher ○ Assistant ○ Administrator ○ Social Worker ○ Occupational Therapist ○ Physiotherapist ○ Speech Pathologist ○ Psychologist ○ Other, _____			
SMART Goal #	○ 1 ○ 2 ○ 3 ○ 4 ○ 5 ○ 6 ○ 7 ○ 8 ○ 9 ○ 10				Short Term Learning Objective	○ 1 ○ 2 ○ 3 ○ 4	Objective or goal met? ○ Y ○ N	

Briefly describe instructional Strategy

Level of Performance (how well did the student perform the activity, from 1 *poor* to 5 *very good*)	○ 1 ○ 2 ○ 3 ○ 4 ○ 5

Briefly describe observed strengths, successes and / or growth

What would you do differently when doing a similar activity related to the above SMART goal, to give the student more opportunities to progress?

What can the Parents / Guardians do at home to support this goal?

Anecdotal Notes and Comments from School Staff

Anecdotal Notes and Comments from Parents / Guardians

Page _____

Today's Date		Start time		End time	
Who worked with the student? (name)			○ Intervention Teacher ○ Classroom Teacher ○ Assistant ○ Administrator ○ Social Worker ○ Occupational Therapist ○ Physiotherapist ○ Speech Pathologist ○ Psychologist ○ Other, _____		
SMART Goal #	○ 1 ○ 2 ○ 3 ○ 4 ○ 5 ○ 6 ○ 7 ○ 8 ○ 9 ○ 10	Short Term Learning Objective	○ 1 ○ 2 ○ 3 ○ 4	Objective or goal met? ○ Y ○ N	

Briefly describe instructional Strategy

Level of Performance (how well did the student perform the activity, from 1 *poor* to 5 *very good*)	○ 1 ○ 2 ○ 3 ○ 4 ○ 5

Briefly describe observed strengths, successes and / or growth

What would you do differently when doing a similar activity related to the above SMART goal, to give the student more opportunities to progress?

What can the Parents / Guardians do at home to support this goal?

Anecdotal Notes and Comments from School Staff

Anecdotal Notes and Comments from Parents / Guardians

Page _____

Today's Date		Start time		End time	
Who worked with the student? (name)		○ Intervention Teacher ○ Classroom Teacher ○ Assistant ○ Administrator ○ Social Worker ○ Occupational Therapist ○ Physiotherapist ○ Speech Pathologist ○ Psychologist ○ Other, _____			
SMART Goal #	○ 1 ○ 2 ○ 3 ○ 4 ○ 5 ○ 6 ○ 7 ○ 8 ○ 9 ○ 10	Short Term Learning Objective	○ 1 ○ 2 ○ 3 ○ 4	Objective or goal met? ○ Y ○ N	

Briefly describe instructional Strategy

Level of Performance (how well did the student perform the activity, from 1 *poor* to 5 *very good*)	○ 1 ○ 2 ○ 3 ○ 4 ○ 5

Briefly describe observed strengths, successes and / or growth

What would you do differently when doing a similar activity related to the above SMART goal, to give the student more opportunities to progress?

What can the Parents / Guardians do at home to support this goal?

Anecdotal Notes and Comments from School Staff

Anecdotal Notes and Comments from Parents / Guardians

Page _____

Today's Date		Start time		End time	
Who worked with the student? (name)			○ Intervention Teacher ○ Classroom Teacher ○ Assistant ○ Administrator ○ Social Worker ○ Occupational Therapist ○ Physiotherapist ○ Speech Pathologist ○ Psychologist ○ Other, _____		
SMART Goal #	○ 1 ○ 2 ○ 3 ○ 4 ○ 5 ○ 6 ○ 7 ○ 8 ○ 9 ○ 10	Short Term Learning Objective	○ 1 ○ 2 ○ 3 ○ 4	Objective or goal met?	○ Y ○ N

Briefly describe instructional Strategy

Level of Performance (how well did the student perform the activity, from 1 *poor* to 5 *very good*)	○ 1 ○ 2 ○ 3 ○ 4 ○ 5

Briefly describe observed strengths, successes and / or growth

What would you do differently when doing a similar activity related to the above SMART goal, to give the student more opportunities to progress?

What can the Parents / Guardians do at home to support this goal?

Anecdotal Notes and Comments from School Staff

Anecdotal Notes and Comments from Parents / Guardians

Page _____

Today's Date		Start time		End time	
Who worked with the student? (name)			○ Intervention Teacher ○ Classroom Teacher ○ Assistant ○ Administrator ○ Social Worker ○ Occupational Therapist ○ Physiotherapist ○ Speech Pathologist ○ Psychologist ○ Other, _____		
SMART Goal #	○ 1 ○ 2 ○ 3 ○ 4 ○ 5 ○ 6 ○ 7 ○ 8 ○ 9 ○ 10	Short Term Learning Objective	○ 1 ○ 2 ○ 3 ○ 4	Objective or goal met? ○ Y ○ N	

Briefly describe instructional Strategy

Level of Performance (how well did the student perform the activity, from 1 *poor* to 5 *very good*)	○ 1 ○ 2 ○ 3 ○ 4 ○ 5

Briefly describe observed strengths, successes and / or growth

What would you do differently when doing a similar activity related to the above SMART goal, to give the student more opportunities to progress?

What can the Parents / Guardians do at home to support this goal?

Anecdotal Notes and Comments from School Staff

Anecdotal Notes and Comments from Parents / Guardians

Page _____

Today's Date		Start time		End time	
Who worked with the student? (name)			○ Intervention Teacher ○ Classroom Teacher ○ Assistant ○ Administrator ○ Social Worker ○ Occupational Therapist ○ Physiotherapist ○ Speech Pathologist ○ Psychologist ○ Other, _____		
SMART Goal #	○ 1 ○ 2 ○ 3 ○ 4 ○ 5 ○ 6 ○ 7 ○ 8 ○ 9 ○ 10	Short Term Learning Objective	○ 1 ○ 2 ○ 3 ○ 4	Objective or goal met? ○ Y ○ N	

Briefly describe instructional Strategy

Level of Performance (how well did the student perform the activity, from 1 *poor* to 5 *very good*)	○ 1 ○ 2 ○ 3 ○ 4 ○ 5

Briefly describe observed strengths, successes and / or growth

What would you do differently when doing a similar activity related to the above SMART goal, to give the student more opportunities to progress?

What can the Parents / Guardians do at home to support this goal?

Anecdotal Notes and Comments from School Staff

Anecdotal Notes and Comments from Parents / Guardians

Page _____

Today's Date		Start time		End time	
Who worked with the student? (name)			○ Intervention Teacher ○ Classroom Teacher ○ Assistant ○ Administrator ○ Social Worker ○ Occupational Therapist ○ Physiotherapist ○ Speech Pathologist ○ Psychologist ○ Other, _____		
SMART Goal #	○ 1 ○ 2 ○ 3 ○ 4 ○ 5 ○ 6 ○ 7 ○ 8 ○ 9 ○ 10	Short Term Learning Objective	○ 1 ○ 2 ○ 3 ○ 4	Objective or goal met? ○ Y ○ N	

Briefly describe instructional Strategy

Level of Performance (how well did the student perform the activity, from 1 *poor* to 5 *very good*)	○ 1 ○ 2 ○ 3 ○ 4 ○ 5

Briefly describe observed strengths, successes and / or growth

What would you do differently when doing a similar activity related to the above SMART goal, to give the student more opportunities to progress?

What can the Parents / Guardians do at home to support this goal?

Anecdotal Notes and Comments from School Staff

Anecdotal Notes and Comments from Parents / Guardians

Page _____

Today's Date		Start time		End time	
Who worked with the student? (name)			○ Intervention Teacher ○ Classroom Teacher ○ Assistant ○ Administrator ○ Social Worker ○ Occupational Therapist ○ Physiotherapist ○ Speech Pathologist ○ Psychologist ○ Other, _____		
SMART Goal #	○ 1 ○ 2 ○ 3 ○ 4 ○ 5 ○ 6 ○ 7 ○ 8 ○ 9 ○ 10	Short Term Learning Objective	○ 1 ○ 2 ○ 3 ○ 4	Objective or goal met? ○ Y ○ N	

Briefly describe instructional Strategy

Level of Performance (how well did the student perform the activity, from 1 *poor* to 5 *very good*)	○ 1 ○ 2 ○ 3 ○ 4 ○ 5

Briefly describe observed strengths, successes and / or growth

What would you do differently when doing a similar activity related to the above SMART goal, to give the student more opportunities to progress?

What can the Parents / Guardians do at home to support this goal?

Anecdotal Notes and Comments from School Staff

Anecdotal Notes and Comments from Parents / Guardians

Page _____

Today's Date		Start time		End time	
Who worked with the student? (name)			○ Intervention Teacher ○ Classroom Teacher ○ Assistant ○ Administrator ○ Social Worker ○ Occupational Therapist ○ Physiotherapist ○ Speech Pathologist ○ Psychologist ○ Other, _____		
SMART Goal #	○ 1 ○ 2 ○ 3 ○ 4 ○ 5 ○ 6 ○ 7 ○ 8 ○ 9 ○ 10	Short Term Learning Objective	○ 1 ○ 2 ○ 3 ○ 4	Objective or goal met? ○ Y ○ N	

Briefly describe instructional Strategy

Level of Performance (how well did the student perform the activity, from 1 *poor* to 5 *very good*)	○ 1 ○ 2 ○ 3 ○ 4 ○ 5

Briefly describe observed strengths, successes and / or growth

What would you do differently when doing a similar activity related to the above SMART goal, to give the student more opportunities to progress?

What can the Parents / Guardians do at home to support this goal?

Anecdotal Notes and Comments from School Staff

Anecdotal Notes and Comments from Parents / Guardians

Page _____

Today's Date		Start time		End time	
Who worked with the student? (name)			○ Intervention Teacher ○ Classroom Teacher ○ Assistant ○ Administrator ○ Social Worker ○ Occupational Therapist ○ Physiotherapist ○ Speech Pathologist ○ Psychologist ○ Other, _____		
SMART Goal #	○ 1 ○ 2 ○ 3 ○ 4 ○ 5 ○ 6 ○ 7 ○ 8 ○ 9 ○ 10	Short Term Learning Objective	○ 1 ○ 2 ○ 3 ○ 4	Objective or goal met? ○ Y ○ N	

Briefly describe instructional Strategy

Level of Performance (how well did the student perform the activity, from 1 *poor* to 5 *very good*)	○ 1 ○ 2 ○ 3 ○ 4 ○ 5

Briefly describe observed strengths, successes and / or growth

What would you do differently when doing a similar activity related to the above SMART goal, to give the student more opportunities to progress?

What can the Parents / Guardians do at home to support this goal?

Anecdotal Notes and Comments from School Staff

Anecdotal Notes and Comments from Parents / Guardians

Today's Date		Start time		End time	
Who worked with the student? (name)			○ Intervention Teacher ○ Classroom Teacher ○ Assistant ○ Administrator ○ Social Worker ○ Occupational Therapist ○ Physiotherapist ○ Speech Pathologist ○ Psychologist ○ Other, _____		
SMART Goal #	○ 1 ○ 2 ○ 3 ○ 4 ○ 5 ○ 6 ○ 7 ○ 8 ○ 9 ○ 10	Short Term Learning Objective	○ 1 ○ 2 ○ 3 ○ 4	Objective or goal met? ○ Y ○ N	

Briefly describe instructional Strategy

Level of Performance (how well did the student perform the activity, from 1 *poor* to 5 *very good*) — ○ 1 ○ 2 ○ 3 ○ 4 ○ 5

Briefly describe observed strengths, successes and / or growth

What would you do differently when doing a similar activity related to the above SMART goal, to give the student more opportunities to progress?

What can the Parents / Guardians do at home to support this goal?

Anecdotal Notes and Comments from School Staff

Anecdotal Notes and Comments from Parents / Guardians

Page _____

Today's Date		Start time		End time	
Who worked with the student? (name)			○ Intervention Teacher ○ Classroom Teacher ○ Assistant ○ Administrator ○ Social Worker ○ Occupational Therapist ○ Physiotherapist ○ Speech Pathologist ○ Psychologist ○ Other, _____		
SMART Goal #	○ 1 ○ 2 ○ 3 ○ 4 ○ 5 ○ 6 ○ 7 ○ 8 ○ 9 ○ 10	Short Term Learning Objective	○ 1 ○ 2 ○ 3 ○ 4	Objective or goal met? ○ Y ○ N	

Briefly describe instructional Strategy

Level of Performance (how well did the student perform the activity, from 1 *poor* to 5 *very good*)	○ 1 ○ 2 ○ 3 ○ 4 ○ 5

Briefly describe observed strengths, successes and / or growth

What would you do differently when doing a similar activity related to the above SMART goal, to give the student more opportunities to progress?

What can the Parents / Guardians do at home to support this goal?

Anecdotal Notes and Comments from School Staff

Anecdotal Notes and Comments from Parents / Guardians

Today's Date		Start time		End time	
Who worked with the student? (name)			○ Intervention Teacher ○ Classroom Teacher ○ Assistant ○ Administrator ○ Social Worker ○ Occupational Therapist ○ Physiotherapist ○ Speech Pathologist ○ Psychologist ○ Other, _____		
SMART Goal #	○ 1 ○ 2 ○ 3 ○ 4 ○ 5 ○ 6 ○ 7 ○ 8 ○ 9 ○ 10	Short Term Learning Objective	○ 1 ○ 2 ○ 3 ○ 4	Objective or goal met? ○ Y ○ N	

Briefly describe instructional Strategy

Level of Performance (how well did the student perform the activity, from 1 *poor* to 5 *very good*)	○ 1 ○ 2 ○ 3 ○ 4 ○ 5

Briefly describe observed strengths, successes and / or growth

What would you do differently when doing a similar activity related to the above SMART goal, to give the student more opportunities to progress?

What can the Parents / Guardians do at home to support this goal?

Anecdotal Notes and Comments from School Staff

Anecdotal Notes and Comments from Parents / Guardians

Today's Date		Start time		End time	
Who worked with the student? (name)			○ Intervention Teacher ○ Classroom Teacher ○ Assistant ○ Administrator ○ Social Worker ○ Occupational Therapist ○ Physiotherapist ○ Speech Pathologist ○ Psychologist ○ Other, _____		
SMART Goal #	○ 1 ○ 2 ○ 3 ○ 4 ○ 5 ○ 6 ○ 7 ○ 8 ○ 9 ○ 10		Short Term Learning Objective	○ 1 ○ 2 ○ 3 ○ 4	Objective or goal met? ○ Y ○ N

Briefly describe instructional Strategy

Level of Performance (how well did the student perform the activity, from 1 *poor* to 5 *very good*)	○ 1 ○ 2 ○ 3 ○ 4 ○ 5

Briefly describe observed strengths, successes and / or growth

What would you do differently when doing a similar activity related to the above SMART goal, to give the student more opportunities to progress?

What can the Parents / Guardians do at home to support this goal?

Anecdotal Notes and Comments from School Staff

Anecdotal Notes and Comments from Parents / Guardians

Page _____

Today's Date		Start time		End time	
Who worked with the student? (name)			○ Intervention Teacher ○ Classroom Teacher ○ Assistant ○ Administrator ○ Social Worker ○ Occupational Therapist ○ Physiotherapist ○ Speech Pathologist ○ Psychologist ○ Other, _____		
SMART Goal #	○ 1 ○ 2 ○ 3 ○ 4 ○ 5 ○ 6 ○ 7 ○ 8 ○ 9 ○ 10	Short Term Learning Objective	○ 1 ○ 2 ○ 3 ○ 4	Objective or goal met? ○ Y ○ N	

Briefly describe instructional Strategy

Level of Performance (how well did the student perform the activity, from 1 *poor* to 5 *very good*)	○ 1 ○ 2 ○ 3 ○ 4 ○ 5

Briefly describe observed strengths, successes and / or growth

What would you do differently when doing a similar activity related to the above SMART goal, to give the student more opportunities to progress?

What can the Parents / Guardians do at home to support this goal?

Anecdotal Notes and Comments from School Staff

Anecdotal Notes and Comments from Parents / Guardians

Page _____

Today's Date		Start time		End time	
Who worked with the student? (name)			○ Intervention Teacher ○ Classroom Teacher ○ Assistant ○ Administrator ○ Social Worker ○ Occupational Therapist ○ Physiotherapist ○ Speech Pathologist ○ Psychologist ○ Other, _____		
SMART Goal #	○1 ○2 ○3 ○4 ○5 ○6 ○7 ○8 ○9 ○10	Short Term Learning Objective	○1 ○2 ○3 ○4	Objective or goal met? ○Y ○N	

Briefly describe instructional Strategy	

Level of Performance (how well did the student perform the activity, from 1 *poor* to 5 *very good*)	○1 ○2 ○3 ○4 ○5

Briefly describe observed strengths, successes and / or growth

What would you do differently when doing a similar activity related to the above SMART goal, to give the student more opportunities to progress?

What can the Parents / Guardians do at home to support this goal?

Anecdotal Notes and Comments from School Staff

Anecdotal Notes and Comments from Parents / Guardians

Today's Date		Start time		End time	
Who worked with the student? (name)			○ Intervention Teacher ○ Classroom Teacher ○ Assistant ○ Administrator ○ Social Worker ○ Occupational Therapist ○ Physiotherapist ○ Speech Pathologist ○ Psychologist ○ Other, _____		
SMART Goal #	○ 1 ○ 2 ○ 3 ○ 4 ○ 5 ○ 6 ○ 7 ○ 8 ○ 9 ○ 10	Short Term Learning Objective	○ 1 ○ 2 ○ 3 ○ 4	Objective or goal met? ○ Y ○ N	

Briefly describe instructional Strategy

Level of Performance (how well did the student perform the activity, from 1 *poor* to 5 *very good*)	○ 1 ○ 2 ○ 3 ○ 4 ○ 5

Briefly describe observed strengths, successes and / or growth

What would you do differently when doing a similar activity related to the above SMART goal, to give the student more opportunities to progress?

What can the Parents / Guardians do at home to support this goal?

Anecdotal Notes and Comments from School Staff

Anecdotal Notes and Comments from Parents / Guardians

Today's Date		Start time		End time	
Who worked with the student? (name)			○ Intervention Teacher ○ Classroom Teacher ○ Assistant ○ Administrator ○ Social Worker ○ Occupational Therapist ○ Physiotherapist ○ Speech Pathologist ○ Psychologist ○ Other, _____		
SMART Goal #	○ 1 ○ 2 ○ 3 ○ 4 ○ 5 ○ 6 ○ 7 ○ 8 ○ 9 ○ 10	Short Term Learning Objective	○ 1 ○ 2 ○ 3 ○ 4	Objective or goal met? ○ Y ○ N	

Briefly describe instructional Strategy

Level of Performance (how well did the student perform the activity, from 1 *poor* to 5 *very good*)	○ 1 ○ 2 ○ 3 ○ 4 ○ 5

Briefly describe observed strengths, successes and / or growth

What would you do differently when doing a similar activity related to the above SMART goal, to give the student more opportunities to progress?

What can the Parents / Guardians do at home to support this goal?

Anecdotal Notes and Comments from School Staff

Anecdotal Notes and Comments from Parents / Guardians

Page _____

Today's Date		Start time		End time	
Who worked with the student? (name)			○ Intervention Teacher ○ Classroom Teacher ○ Assistant ○ Administrator ○ Social Worker ○ Occupational Therapist ○ Physiotherapist ○ Speech Pathologist ○ Psychologist ○ Other, _____		
SMART Goal #	○ 1 ○ 2 ○ 3 ○ 4 ○ 5 ○ 6 ○ 7 ○ 8 ○ 9 ○ 10	Short Term Learning Objective	○ 1 ○ 2 ○ 3 ○ 4	Objective or goal met? ○ Y ○ N	

Briefly describe instructional Strategy

Level of Performance (how well did the student perform the activity, from 1 *poor* to 5 *very good*)	○ 1 ○ 2 ○ 3 ○ 4 ○ 5

Briefly describe observed strengths, successes and / or growth

What would you do differently when doing a similar activity related to the above SMART goal, to give the student more opportunities to progress?

What can the Parents / Guardians do at home to support this goal?

Anecdotal Notes and Comments from School Staff

Anecdotal Notes and Comments from Parents / Guardians

Page _____

Today's Date		Start time		End time	
Who worked with the student? (name)			○ Intervention Teacher ○ Classroom Teacher ○ Assistant ○ Administrator ○ Social Worker ○ Occupational Therapist ○ Physiotherapist ○ Speech Pathologist ○ Psychologist ○ Other, _____		
SMART Goal #	○ 1 ○ 2 ○ 3 ○ 4 ○ 5 ○ 6 ○ 7 ○ 8 ○ 9 ○ 10		Short Term Learning Objective	○ 1 ○ 2 ○ 3 ○ 4	Objective or goal met? ○ Y ○ N

Briefly describe instructional Strategy

Level of Performance (how well did the student perform the activity, from 1 *poor* to 5 *very good*)	○ 1 ○ 2 ○ 3 ○ 4 ○ 5

Briefly describe observed strengths, successes and / or growth

What would you do differently when doing a similar activity related to the above SMART goal, to give the student more opportunities to progress?

What can the Parents / Guardians do at home to support this goal?

Anecdotal Notes and Comments from School Staff

Anecdotal Notes and Comments from Parents / Guardians

Page _____

Today's Date		Start time		End time	
Who worked with the student? (name)			○ Intervention Teacher ○ Classroom Teacher ○ Assistant ○ Administrator ○ Social Worker ○ Occupational Therapist ○ Physiotherapist ○ Speech Pathologist ○ Psychologist ○ Other, _____		
SMART Goal #	○ 1 ○ 2 ○ 3 ○ 4 ○ 5 ○ 6 ○ 7 ○ 8 ○ 9 ○ 10	Short Term Learning Objective	○ 1 ○ 2 ○ 3 ○ 4	Objective or goal met?	○ Y ○ N

Briefly describe instructional Strategy

Level of Performance (how well did the student perform the activity, from 1 *poor* to 5 *very good*) — ○ 1 ○ 2 ○ 3 ○ 4 ○ 5

Briefly describe observed strengths, successes and / or growth

What would you do differently when doing a similar activity related to the above SMART goal, to give the student more opportunities to progress?

What can the Parents / Guardians do at home to support this goal?

Anecdotal Notes and Comments from School Staff

Anecdotal Notes and Comments from Parents / Guardians

Today's Date		Start time		End time	
Who worked with the student? (name)			○ Intervention Teacher ○ Classroom Teacher ○ Assistant ○ Administrator ○ Social Worker ○ Occupational Therapist ○ Physiotherapist ○ Speech Pathologist ○ Psychologist ○ Other, _____		
SMART Goal #	○1 ○2 ○3 ○4 ○5 ○6 ○7 ○8 ○9 ○10		Short Term Learning Objective	○1 ○2 ○3 ○4	Objective or goal met? ○Y ○N

Briefly describe instructional Strategy

Level of Performance (how well did the student perform the activity, from 1 *poor* to 5 *very good*)	○1 ○2 ○3 ○4 ○5

Briefly describe observed strengths, successes and / or growth

What would you do differently when doing a similar activity related to the above SMART goal, to give the student more opportunities to progress?

What can the Parents / Guardians do at home to support this goal?

Anecdotal Notes and Comments from School Staff

Anecdotal Notes and Comments from Parents / Guardians

Page _____

Today's Date		Start time		End time	
Who worked with the student? (name)			○ Intervention Teacher ○ Classroom Teacher ○ Assistant ○ Administrator ○ Social Worker ○ Occupational Therapist ○ Physiotherapist ○ Speech Pathologist ○ Psychologist ○ Other, _____		
SMART Goal #	○ 1 ○ 2 ○ 3 ○ 4 ○ 5 ○ 6 ○ 7 ○ 8 ○ 9 ○ 10	Short Term Learning Objective	○ 1 ○ 2 ○ 3 ○ 4	Objective or goal met? ○ Y ○ N	

Briefly describe instructional Strategy

Level of Performance (how well did the student perform the activity, from 1 *poor* to 5 *very good*)	○ 1 ○ 2 ○ 3 ○ 4 ○ 5

Briefly describe observed strengths, successes and / or growth

What would you do differently when doing a similar activity related to the above SMART goal, to give the student more opportunities to progress?

What can the Parents / Guardians do at home to support this goal?

Anecdotal Notes and Comments from School Staff

Anecdotal Notes and Comments from Parents / Guardians

Today's Date		Start time		End time	
Who worked with the student? (name)		○ Intervention Teacher ○ Classroom Teacher ○ Assistant ○ Administrator ○ Social Worker ○ Occupational Therapist ○ Physiotherapist ○ Speech Pathologist ○ Psychologist ○ Other, _____			
SMART Goal #	○ 1 ○ 2 ○ 3 ○ 4 ○ 5 ○ 6 ○ 7 ○ 8 ○ 9 ○ 10	Short Term Learning Objective	○ 1 ○ 2 ○ 3 ○ 4	Objective or goal met?	○ Y ○ N

Briefly describe instructional Strategy

Level of Performance (how well did the student perform the activity, from 1 *poor* to 5 *very good*) — ○ 1 ○ 2 ○ 3 ○ 4 ○ 5

Briefly describe observed strengths, successes and / or growth

What would you do differently when doing a similar activity related to the above SMART goal, to give the student more opportunities to progress?

What can the Parents / Guardians do at home to support this goal?

Anecdotal Notes and Comments from School Staff

Anecdotal Notes and Comments from Parents / Guardians

Page _____

Today's Date		Start time		End time	
Who worked with the student? (name)			○ Intervention Teacher ○ Classroom Teacher ○ Assistant ○ Administrator ○ Social Worker ○ Occupational Therapist ○ Physiotherapist ○ Speech Pathologist ○ Psychologist ○ Other, _____		
SMART Goal #	○ 1 ○ 2 ○ 3 ○ 4 ○ 5 ○ 6 ○ 7 ○ 8 ○ 9 ○ 10	Short Term Learning Objective	○ 1 ○ 2 ○ 3 ○ 4	Objective or goal met?	○ Y ○ N

Briefly describe instructional Strategy

Level of Performance (how well did the student perform the activity, from 1 *poor* to 5 *very good*)	○ 1 ○ 2 ○ 3 ○ 4 ○ 5

Briefly describe observed strengths, successes and / or growth

What would you do differently when doing a similar activity related to the above SMART goal, to give the student more opportunities to progress?

What can the Parents / Guardians do at home to support this goal?

Anecdotal Notes and Comments from School Staff

Anecdotal Notes and Comments from Parents / Guardians

Page _____

Today's Date		Start time		End time	
Who worked with the student? (name)			○ Intervention Teacher ○ Classroom Teacher ○ Assistant ○ Administrator ○ Social Worker ○ Occupational Therapist ○ Physiotherapist ○ Speech Pathologist ○ Psychologist ○ Other, _____		
SMART Goal #	○ 1 ○ 2 ○ 3 ○ 4 ○ 5 ○ 6 ○ 7 ○ 8 ○ 9 ○ 10	Short Term Learning Objective	○ 1 ○ 2 ○ 3 ○ 4	Objective or goal met? ○ Y ○ N	

Briefly describe instructional Strategy

Level of Performance (how well did the student perform the activity, from 1 *poor* to 5 *very good*)	○ 1 ○ 2 ○ 3 ○ 4 ○ 5

Briefly describe observed strengths, successes and / or growth

What would you do differently when doing a similar activity related to the above SMART goal, to give the student more opportunities to progress?

What can the Parents / Guardians do at home to support this goal?

Anecdotal Notes and Comments from School Staff

Anecdotal Notes and Comments from Parents / Guardians

Page _____

Today's Date		Start time		End time	
Who worked with the student? (name)			○ Intervention Teacher ○ Classroom Teacher ○ Assistant ○ Administrator ○ Social Worker ○ Occupational Therapist ○ Physiotherapist ○ Speech Pathologist ○ Psychologist ○ Other, _____		
SMART Goal #	○ 1 ○ 2 ○ 3 ○ 4 ○ 5 ○ 6 ○ 7 ○ 8 ○ 9 ○ 10	Short Term Learning Objective	○ 1 ○ 2 ○ 3 ○ 4	Objective or goal met?	○ Y ○ N

Briefly describe instructional Strategy

Level of Performance (how well did the student perform the activity, from 1 *poor* to 5 *very good*)	○ 1 ○ 2 ○ 3 ○ 4 ○ 5

Briefly describe observed strengths, successes and / or growth

What would you do differently when doing a similar activity related to the above SMART goal, to give the student more opportunities to progress?

What can the Parents / Guardians do at home to support this goal?

Anecdotal Notes and Comments from School Staff

Anecdotal Notes and Comments from Parents / Guardians

Page _____

Today's Date		Start time		End time	
Who worked with the student? (name)			○ Intervention Teacher ○ Classroom Teacher ○ Assistant ○ Administrator ○ Social Worker ○ Occupational Therapist ○ Physiotherapist ○ Speech Pathologist ○ Psychologist ○ Other, _____		
SMART Goal #	○ 1 ○ 2 ○ 3 ○ 4 ○ 5 ○ 6 ○ 7 ○ 8 ○ 9 ○ 10	Short Term Learning Objective	○ 1 ○ 2 ○ 3 ○ 4	Objective or goal met? ○ Y ○ N	

Briefly describe instructional Strategy

Level of Performance (how well did the student perform the activity, from 1 *poor* to 5 *very good*)	○ 1 ○ 2 ○ 3 ○ 4 ○ 5

Briefly describe observed strengths, successes and / or growth

What would you do differently when doing a similar activity related to the above SMART goal, to give the student more opportunities to progress?

What can the Parents / Guardians do at home to support this goal?

Anecdotal Notes and Comments from School Staff

Anecdotal Notes and Comments from Parents / Guardians

Page _____

Today's Date		Start time		End time	
Who worked with the student? (name)			○ Intervention Teacher ○ Classroom Teacher ○ Assistant ○ Administrator ○ Social Worker ○ Occupational Therapist ○ Physiotherapist ○ Speech Pathologist ○ Psychologist ○ Other, _____		
SMART Goal #	○ 1 ○ 2 ○ 3 ○ 4 ○ 5 ○ 6 ○ 7 ○ 8 ○ 9 ○ 10	Short Term Learning Objective	○ 1 ○ 2 ○ 3 ○ 4	Objective or goal met?	○ Y ○ N

Briefly describe instructional Strategy

Level of Performance (how well did the student perform the activity, from 1 *poor* to 5 *very good*)	○ 1 ○ 2 ○ 3 ○ 4 ○ 5

Briefly describe observed strengths, successes and / or growth

What would you do differently when doing a similar activity related to the above SMART goal, to give the student more opportunities to progress?

What can the Parents / Guardians do at home to support this goal?

Anecdotal Notes and Comments from School Staff

Anecdotal Notes and Comments from Parents / Guardians

Page _____

Today's Date		Start time		End time	
Who worked with the student? (name)			○ Intervention Teacher ○ Classroom Teacher ○ Assistant ○ Administrator ○ Social Worker ○ Occupational Therapist ○ Physiotherapist ○ Speech Pathologist ○ Psychologist ○ Other, _____		
SMART Goal #	○ 1 ○ 2 ○ 3 ○ 4 ○ 5 ○ 6 ○ 7 ○ 8 ○ 9 ○ 10	Short Term Learning Objective	○ 1 ○ 2 ○ 3 ○ 4	Objective or goal met? ○ Y ○ N	

Briefly describe instructional Strategy

Level of Performance (how well did the student perform the activity, from 1 *poor* to 5 *very good*)	○ 1 ○ 2 ○ 3 ○ 4 ○ 5

Briefly describe observed strengths, successes and / or growth

What would you do differently when doing a similar activity related to the above SMART goal, to give the student more opportunities to progress?

What can the Parents / Guardians do at home to support this goal?

Anecdotal Notes and Comments from School Staff

Anecdotal Notes and Comments from Parents / Guardians

Page _____

Today's Date		Start time		End time	
Who worked with the student? (name)			○ Intervention Teacher ○ Classroom Teacher ○ Assistant ○ Administrator ○ Social Worker ○ Occupational Therapist ○ Physiotherapist ○ Speech Pathologist ○ Psychologist ○ Other, _____		
SMART Goal #	○ 1 ○ 2 ○ 3 ○ 4 ○ 5 ○ 6 ○ 7 ○ 8 ○ 9 ○ 10	Short Term Learning Objective	○ 1 ○ 2 ○ 3 ○ 4	Objective or goal met? ○ Y ○ N	

Briefly describe instructional Strategy

Level of Performance (how well did the student perform the activity, from 1 *poor* to 5 *very good*) ○ 1 ○ 2 ○ 3 ○ 4 ○ 5

Briefly describe observed strengths, successes and / or growth

What would you do differently when doing a similar activity related to the above SMART goal, to give the student more opportunities to progress?

What can the Parents / Guardians do at home to support this goal?

Anecdotal Notes and Comments from School Staff

Anecdotal Notes and Comments from Parents / Guardians

Page _____

Today's Date		Start time		End time	
Who worked with the student? (name)			○ Intervention Teacher ○ Classroom Teacher ○ Assistant ○ Administrator ○ Social Worker ○ Occupational Therapist ○ Physiotherapist ○ Speech Pathologist ○ Psychologist ○ Other, _____		
SMART Goal #	○ 1 ○ 2 ○ 3 ○ 4 ○ 5 ○ 6 ○ 7 ○ 8 ○ 9 ○ 10		Short Term Learning Objective	○ 1 ○ 2 ○ 3 ○ 4	Objective or goal met? ○ Y ○ N

Briefly describe instructional Strategy

Level of Performance (how well did the student perform the activity, from 1 *poor* to 5 *very good*)	○ 1 ○ 2 ○ 3 ○ 4 ○ 5

Briefly describe observed strengths, successes and / or growth

What would you do differently when doing a similar activity related to the above SMART goal, to give the student more opportunities to progress?

What can the Parents / Guardians do at home to support this goal?

Anecdotal Notes and Comments from School Staff

Anecdotal Notes and Comments from Parents / Guardians

Page _____

Today's Date		Start time		End time	
Who worked with the student? (name)			○ Intervention Teacher ○ Classroom Teacher ○ Assistant ○ Administrator ○ Social Worker ○ Occupational Therapist ○ Physiotherapist ○ Speech Pathologist ○ Psychologist ○ Other, _____		
SMART Goal #	○1 ○2 ○3 ○4 ○5 ○6 ○7 ○8 ○9 ○10	Short Term Learning Objective	○1 ○2 ○3 ○4	Objective or goal met? ○Y ○N	

Briefly describe instructional Strategy

Level of Performance (how well did the student perform the activity, from 1 *poor* to 5 *very good*)	○1 ○2 ○3 ○4 ○5

Briefly describe observed strengths, successes and / or growth

What would you do differently when doing a similar activity related to the above SMART goal, to give the student more opportunities to progress?

What can the Parents / Guardians do at home to support this goal?

Anecdotal Notes and Comments from School Staff

Anecdotal Notes and Comments from Parents / Guardians

Page _____

Today's Date		Start time		End time	
Who worked with the student? (name)			○ Intervention Teacher ○ Classroom Teacher ○ Assistant ○ Administrator ○ Social Worker ○ Occupational Therapist ○ Physiotherapist ○ Speech Pathologist ○ Psychologist ○ Other, _____		
SMART Goal #	○ 1 ○ 2 ○ 3 ○ 4 ○ 5 ○ 6 ○ 7 ○ 8 ○ 9 ○ 10		Short Term Learning Objective	○ 1 ○ 2 ○ 3 ○ 4	Objective or goal met? ○ Y ○ N

Briefly describe instructional Strategy

Level of Performance (how well did the student perform the activity, from 1 *poor* to 5 *very good*)	○ 1 ○ 2 ○ 3 ○ 4 ○ 5

Briefly describe observed strengths, successes and / or growth

What would you do differently when doing a similar activity related to the above SMART goal, to give the student more opportunities to progress?

What can the Parents / Guardians do at home to support this goal?

Anecdotal Notes and Comments from School Staff

Anecdotal Notes and Comments from Parents / Guardians

Page _____

Today's Date		Start time		End time	
Who worked with the student? (name)			○ Intervention Teacher ○ Classroom Teacher ○ Assistant ○ Administrator ○ Social Worker ○ Occupational Therapist ○ Physiotherapist ○ Speech Pathologist ○ Psychologist ○ Other, _____		
SMART Goal #	○ 1 ○ 2 ○ 3 ○ 4 ○ 5 ○ 6 ○ 7 ○ 8 ○ 9 ○ 10	Short Term Learning Objective	○ 1 ○ 2 ○ 3 ○ 4	Objective or goal met?	○ Y ○ N

Briefly describe instructional Strategy

Level of Performance (how well did the student perform the activity, from 1 *poor* to 5 *very good*)	○ 1 ○ 2 ○ 3 ○ 4 ○ 5

Briefly describe observed strengths, successes and / or growth

What would you do differently when doing a similar activity related to the above SMART goal, to give the student more opportunities to progress?

What can the Parents / Guardians do at home to support this goal?

Anecdotal Notes and Comments from School Staff

Anecdotal Notes and Comments from Parents / Guardians

Page _____

Today's Date		Start time		End time	
Who worked with the student? (name)			○ Intervention Teacher ○ Classroom Teacher ○ Assistant ○ Administrator ○ Social Worker ○ Occupational Therapist ○ Physiotherapist ○ Speech Pathologist ○ Psychologist ○ Other, _____		
SMART Goal #	○ 1 ○ 2 ○ 3 ○ 4 ○ 5 ○ 6 ○ 7 ○ 8 ○ 9 ○ 10	Short Term Learning Objective	○ 1 ○ 2 ○ 3 ○ 4	Objective or goal met? ○ Y ○ N	

Briefly describe instructional Strategy

Level of Performance (how well did the student perform the activity, from 1 *poor* to 5 *very good*)	○ 1 ○ 2 ○ 3 ○ 4 ○ 5

Briefly describe observed strengths, successes and / or growth

What would you do differently when doing a similar activity related to the above SMART goal, to give the student more opportunities to progress?

What can the Parents / Guardians do at home to support this goal?

Anecdotal Notes and Comments from School Staff

Anecdotal Notes and Comments from Parents / Guardians

Page _____

Today's Date		Start time		End time	
Who worked with the student? (name)		○ Intervention Teacher ○ Classroom Teacher ○ Assistant ○ Administrator ○ Social Worker ○ Occupational Therapist ○ Physiotherapist ○ Speech Pathologist ○ Psychologist ○ Other, _____			
SMART Goal #	○ 1 ○ 2 ○ 3 ○ 4 ○ 5 ○ 6 ○ 7 ○ 8 ○ 9 ○ 10	Short Term Learning Objective	○ 1 ○ 2 ○ 3 ○ 4	Objective or goal met?	○ Y ○ N

Briefly describe instructional Strategy

Level of Performance (how well did the student perform the activity, from 1 *poor* to 5 *very good*)	○ 1 ○ 2 ○ 3 ○ 4 ○ 5

Briefly describe observed strengths, successes and / or growth

What would you do differently when doing a similar activity related to the above SMART goal, to give the student more opportunities to progress?

What can the Parents / Guardians do at home to support this goal?

Anecdotal Notes and Comments from School Staff

Anecdotal Notes and Comments from Parents / Guardians

Page _____

Today's Date		Start time		End time	
Who worked with the student? (name)			○ Intervention Teacher ○ Classroom Teacher ○ Assistant ○ Administrator ○ Social Worker ○ Occupational Therapist ○ Physiotherapist ○ Speech Pathologist ○ Psychologist ○ Other, _____		
SMART Goal #	○ 1 ○ 2 ○ 3 ○ 4 ○ 5 ○ 6 ○ 7 ○ 8 ○ 9 ○ 10	Short Term Learning Objective	○ 1 ○ 2 ○ 3 ○ 4	Objective or goal met? ○ Y ○ N	

Briefly describe instructional Strategy

Level of Performance (how well did the student perform the activity, from 1 *poor* to 5 *very good*)	○ 1 ○ 2 ○ 3 ○ 4 ○ 5

Briefly describe observed strengths, successes and / or growth

What would you do differently when doing a similar activity related to the above SMART goal, to give the student more opportunities to progress?

What can the Parents / Guardians do at home to support this goal?

Anecdotal Notes and Comments from School Staff

Anecdotal Notes and Comments from Parents / Guardians

Today's Date		Start time		End time	
Who worked with the student? (name)			○ Intervention Teacher ○ Classroom Teacher ○ Assistant ○ Administrator ○ Social Worker ○ Occupational Therapist ○ Physiotherapist ○ Speech Pathologist ○ Psychologist ○ Other, _____		
SMART Goal #	○ 1 ○ 2 ○ 3 ○ 4 ○ 5 ○ 6 ○ 7 ○ 8 ○ 9 ○ 10	Short Term Learning Objective	○ 1 ○ 2 ○ 3 ○ 4	Objective or goal met?	○ Y ○ N

Briefly describe instructional Strategy

Level of Performance (how well did the student perform the activity, from 1 *poor* to 5 *very good*)	○ 1 ○ 2 ○ 3 ○ 4 ○ 5

Briefly describe observed strengths, successes and / or growth

What would you do differently when doing a similar activity related to the above SMART goal, to give the student more opportunities to progress?

What can the Parents / Guardians do at home to support this goal?

Anecdotal Notes and Comments from School Staff

Anecdotal Notes and Comments from Parents / Guardians

Today's Date		Start time		End time	
Who worked with the student? (name)			○ Intervention Teacher ○ Classroom Teacher ○ Assistant ○ Administrator ○ Social Worker ○ Occupational Therapist ○ Physiotherapist ○ Speech Pathologist ○ Psychologist ○ Other, _____		
SMART Goal #	○ 1 ○ 2 ○ 3 ○ 4 ○ 5 ○ 6 ○ 7 ○ 8 ○ 9 ○ 10	Short Term Learning Objective	○ 1 ○ 2 ○ 3 ○ 4	Objective or goal met? ○ Y ○ N	

Briefly describe instructional Strategy

Level of Performance (how well did the student perform the activity, from 1 *poor* to 5 *very good*)	○ 1 ○ 2 ○ 3 ○ 4 ○ 5

Briefly describe observed strengths, successes and / or growth

---

What would you do differently when doing a similar activity related to the above SMART goal, to give the student more opportunities to progress?

What can the Parents / Guardians do at home to support this goal?

Anecdotal Notes and Comments from School Staff

Anecdotal Notes and Comments from Parents / Guardians

Page _____

Today's Date		Start time		End time	
Who worked with the student? (name)			○ Intervention Teacher ○ Classroom Teacher ○ Assistant ○ Administrator ○ Social Worker ○ Occupational Therapist ○ Physiotherapist ○ Speech Pathologist ○ Psychologist ○ Other, _____		
SMART Goal #	○ 1 ○ 2 ○ 3 ○ 4 ○ 5 ○ 6 ○ 7 ○ 8 ○ 9 ○ 10	Short Term Learning Objective	○ 1 ○ 2 ○ 3 ○ 4	Objective or goal met? ○ Y ○ N	

Briefly describe instructional Strategy

Level of Performance (how well did the student perform the activity, from 1 *poor* to 5 *very good*)	○ 1 ○ 2 ○ 3 ○ 4 ○ 5

Briefly describe observed strengths, successes and / or growth

What would you do differently when doing a similar activity related to the above SMART goal, to give the student more opportunities to progress?

What can the Parents / Guardians do at home to support this goal?

Anecdotal Notes and Comments from School Staff

Anecdotal Notes and Comments from Parents / Guardians

Page _____

Today's Date		Start time		End time	
Who worked with the student? (name)			○ Intervention Teacher ○ Classroom Teacher ○ Assistant ○ Administrator ○ Social Worker ○ Occupational Therapist ○ Physiotherapist ○ Speech Pathologist ○ Psychologist ○ Other, _____		
SMART Goal #	○ 1 ○ 2 ○ 3 ○ 4 ○ 5 ○ 6 ○ 7 ○ 8 ○ 9 ○ 10	Short Term Learning Objective	○ 1 ○ 2 ○ 3 ○ 4	Objective or goal met? ○ Y ○ N	

Briefly describe instructional Strategy

Level of Performance (how well did the student perform the activity, from 1 *poor* to 5 *very good*)	○ 1 ○ 2 ○ 3 ○ 4 ○ 5

Briefly describe observed strengths, successes and / or growth

What would you do differently when doing a similar activity related to the above SMART goal, to give the student more opportunities to progress?

What can the Parents / Guardians do at home to support this goal?

Anecdotal Notes and Comments from School Staff

Anecdotal Notes and Comments from Parents / Guardians

Today's Date		Start time		End time	
Who worked with the student? (name)			○ Intervention Teacher ○ Classroom Teacher ○ Assistant ○ Administrator ○ Social Worker ○ Occupational Therapist ○ Physiotherapist ○ Speech Pathologist ○ Psychologist ○ Other, _____		
SMART Goal #	○ 1 ○ 2 ○ 3 ○ 4 ○ 5 ○ 6 ○ 7 ○ 8 ○ 9 ○ 10	Short Term Learning Objective	○ 1 ○ 2 ○ 3 ○ 4	Objective or goal met? ○ Y ○ N	

Briefly describe instructional Strategy

Level of Performance (how well did the student perform the activity, from 1 *poor* to 5 *very good*)	○ 1 ○ 2 ○ 3 ○ 4 ○ 5

Briefly describe observed strengths, successes and / or growth

What would you do differently when doing a similar activity related to the above SMART goal, to give the student more opportunities to progress?

What can the Parents / Guardians do at home to support this goal?

Anecdotal Notes and Comments from School Staff

Anecdotal Notes and Comments from Parents / Guardians

Page _____

Made in the USA
Middletown, DE
29 March 2019